Journal Buddies

A Boy's Journal for Discovering
and Sharing Excellence

Jill Schoenberg

Published by

Blue Sky at Night Publishing

Jill Schoenberg—

Journal Buddies:

A Boy's Journal for Discovering and Sharing Excellence

ISBN 13: 978-0-9768623-2-1

ISBN 10: 0-9768623-2-8

1. Juvenile Nonfiction   2. Social Situations

3. Self-Esteem & Self-Reliance I. Title

Cover and book design by AuthorSupport.com

This project was made possible, in part, by a grant provided by the Five Wings Arts Council with funds from the McKnight Foundation.

Printed in the United States of America

1 3 5 7 9 10 8 5 4 2

For information regarding special discounts on bulk sales, please contact Jill (the author and creator of this journal) at www.JournalBuddies.com or Jill@JournalBuddies.com.

To Mitchell and Jacob and to every boy on earth.
May you always know how deeply loved you are.

This copy of *Journal Buddies* belongs to:

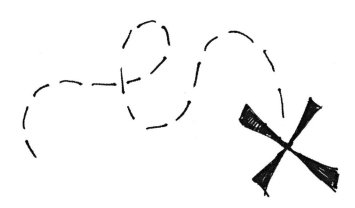

Date Started:

Date Completed:

Table of Contents

What's This All About?

Welcome to *Journal Buddies!* You are at the beginning of a brand new adventure that is all about exploring excellence. That's a neat word, isn't it? Just in case you're not sure how to say the word excellence it sounds like this: X – sah – LINTS. You can say it out loud or simply think about it... X – sah – LINTS. Do you know what it means?

Excellence is the state of being

excellent (X – sah – LINT), as in:

I am excellent.

I am incredible.

I am super-duper cool.

Journal Buddies is all about discovering how excellence feels and about learning what it means to be excellent. On your journaling adventure, you will learn to FOCUS ON and MAGNIFY the positive, excellent characteristics that you like about yourself and others. Why? Because it is SUPER fun to discover and share the stuff that you really love, like or enjoy about yourself and your buddies! And when you practice LOOKING for the good stuff, you will learn how to SEE the good stuff. Your self-esteem and self-confidence will grow stronger and you will enjoy just being YOU even more!

The concept of *Journal Buddies* is simple. Have you ever looked at something through a magnifying glass? Do you remember what happened? Did it suddenly seem bigger? Was it easier to see? Were the details more clear and obvious? You are like that — you're like a magnifying glass. And whatever you focus on grows bigger! So do you want to see what happens when you focus on excellence? Well, that's what this journal is all about...

Three Basic Parts

How does *Journal Buddies* work? There are three basic parts to help you along in your journaling adventure. They are:

Part 1 Sharing Your Journal
Part 2 Creative Journaling
Part 3 Kindness

The next few pages describe these three parts. So come on, keep reading to find out more about these super-cool and unique aspects of *Journal Buddies*! You'll be really glad you did. I promise.

Part 1 Sharing Your Journal

Journal Buddies is no ordinary journal. It's about stuff like discovering treasures and sharing them with others, and it's about creativity, kindness, and building your self-esteem too. But one of the most unique features of this journal is that it's shared! This means that YOU complete the journal entries with the help of your buddies.

Inside *Journal Buddies*, you will find thirty different journal entries, or one for each day, for about a month. You will need a journal buddy to help you uncover your excellent discoveries and to complete each entry. You can choose the same buddy for each day, or a few different buddies to help you with the book, or a new buddy each and every time! It's your choice.

Your buddy could be a friend from school, or a grandparent that you call on the phone. You could choose a parent, a brother or sister, a cousin, your uncle, a mentor, your neighbor or a teacher. You could even choose your cat or your dog, your hamster or your imaginary friend to be your journal buddy! And you can do *Journal Buddies* with someone who has the book or with someone who doesn't have it — it works both ways.

Take a moment and see who comes to mind when you think about your journal buddies. Make a list and write their names below. You can add to this list later if you think of more buddies.

1. ....

2. ....

3. ....

4. ....

5. ....

6. ....

7. ....

8. ....

9. ....

10. ....

11. ....

12. ....

13. ....

14. ....

15. ....

Sharing your excellent discoveries is just one part of the unforgettable journaling adventure that you're about to experience! Let's check out the next part.

Part 2 Creative Journaling

I want to introduce you to something really fun and exciting. It's SO fun and exciting that I think once you try it a few times, you'll want to finish this journal all the way to the end! Are you ready? It's called creative journaling, and it allows you to personalize your journal to YOUR style and your unique personality.

I want you to make your journaling experience as fun and exciting as possible, but to do this you'll need to be creative! And believe me, absolutely everyone is creative in some way! Take a moment and think about the following questions.

Do you enjoy writing, drawing or painting?

Do you like cutting things out and then pasting them onto a page?

Do you like stickers or stamps or photographs?

You can use one of these ideas for your creative journaling or some of the ideas or ALL of them. It's your journal and your choice. This is so important that I am going to say it again — it's YOUR CHOICE how you keep this journal! You might choose to add color and creative flair to your journal by writing in it with markers, colored pencils or even crayons. If you prefer, you may choose to cut out pictures from a magazine or from a newspaper and paste them into your journal to make a collage. Or you could use pictures of your friends and family. You might even choose to write a single word across a whole page in gigantic letters! I hope you see where I'm going with this idea of creative journaling. It sounds fun, doesn't it?

If you need some help getting started, check out the list of ideas on pages 24 - 31. And remember, you can ALWAYS make up your own creative journaling ideas too.

Part 3 Kindness

Have you ever thought something kind about someone and felt silly, embarrassed or even ashamed for thinking about it? What about yourself? How many times have you felt sort of weird and uncomfortable when thinking of the really great stuff about yourself? Well I'm here to tell you that it's okay to feel really proud of who you are! It's also really fun to give, share and receive kindness — it feels outrageously good, especially after you practice for a while and feel comfortable doing it. And, by the way... it is cool for boys to be kind to themselves and to others.

So in addition to completing this journal with the help of a buddy — or many buddies — and using creative journaling techniques, you're going to learn how to practice kindness. You will practice kindness by looking for and finding the stuff that you like about yourself and others and then sharing what you SEE.

By completing all thirty journal entries, you create the healthy habit of focusing on the positives and practicing kindness. When you focus on the positives and focus on kindness, you feel better about yourself. And when you feel better about yourself, your self-esteem and self-confidence increases and your excellence expands! It's as simple as that.

Let's Review

I hope that by now you're starting to get excited about using this journal! Before we go on, let's review what we've learned about *Journal Buddies* so far.

First of all, it is shared and interactive, which means that you complete the journal with the help of others — parents, friends, siblings, teachers, mentors or anyone else of your choice. Second, you're encouraged to discover your own creative style and to make this journal a one-of-a-kind, unique expression of YOU. That's what creative journaling is all about! Finally, you're going to look for the qualities, traits and talents that you admire in your buddies. And you're going practice kindness, by telling them what you see! Basically, the formula looks like this:

As you complete this journal, you'll be amazed by how many wonderful things you discover about your excellent self and your excellent buddies! Oh, and I bet that you'll also be thrilled by all of your creative journaling ideas and how fantastic it feels to share kindness. Most of all, make sure that you have loads of fun along the way!

Sometimes We Don't Feel Excellent

This book is about discovering how excellence feels and about learning what it means to be excellent. Of course sometimes we don't feel excellent or we don't feel good and it's really important to pay attention to that stuff too.

If you feel hurt or angry or stressed out, talk to a grown-up about it. If something is happening in your life that seems wrong, hurtful, unfair or feels bad, find someone that you trust and ask them to help you. If you're being bullied, criticizing yourself a lot, or feeling depressed or unhappy, reach out to an adult who can help you. Am I being clear here? Even though it may be scary to talk about, it is very important for you to get someone to help you through your difficult time! Even grown-ups ask for help when they're having a hard time. And if the first person you ask doesn't help you enough, try someone else. Keep speaking up until you find someone who can help you feel excellent again... you can do it. I know you can!

Whether you're feeling good or bad, just do your best. That's good enough! And when you're having a hard day, try to focus on what you like or enjoy about yourself and others. Do this for at least a little while – or for a long while, whichever feels the best to you. Just remember, do your best to try and celebrate the positive in some way, everyday! Because no matter what is going on in your life, good or bad, you're still amazing in a gazillion different ways. And that's the truth!

A Very Special Message from the Creator of Journal Buddies, especially for You!

Some people have said to me "boys don't journal!" and my response to them is "YES, THEY DO!" Believe it or not, lots of boys actually journal all the time. You might even be one of those boys and not realize it! Think about the following:

- When you sketch on scrap paper – or on your homework – you're journaling.

- When you draw cartoons or doodle cool designs, you're journaling.

- When you find yourself randomly scribbling words across a page or creating a song or a poem or a story, well... that's journaling too!

See what I mean? It's very likely that you already journal a lot in some form and you just don't call it journaling. In fact, it's very likely that you have sketched, drawn, or written something on paper sometime in the last few days. Did you? What was it? Take a minute to think about it – maybe you wrote a song, or maybe you doodled on a scrap piece of paper. Just remember this very important point: journaling – in any form – helps you to discover who you are and what it is that makes you stand out from the crowd. AND that's EXACTLY what *Journal Buddies* is all about!

I also want you to know that this journal is not about seeking approval or pleasing others. It is about giving yourself permission to practice kindness and creative expression with yourself and with your buddies. It's about DISCOVERING AND SHARING! This journal is also about building a positive outlook, strengthening your self-esteem, and increasing self-confidence as you become more and more aware of all of your excellent qualities, traits and talents. Remember, what we focus on grows bigger!

I want you to see this journal as a safe, fun and enjoyable place for you to practice being kind to yourself and to others, and also to explore your creativity. I want you to use this journal only if you WANT to – not because you HAVE to or because you're being told to. Find ways to make it your own, to make it really work for YOU! If you choose to complete this journal, here's what I think will happen: you'll begin to feel stronger and braver day by day, and your kindness and creativity will expand too. You might even strengthen your character so much that the day will come when you will be able to be kind to anyone, anyplace, regardless of what they are doing. You may also become brave enough to openly share your excellent self with anyone, anywhere, anytime! What an amazing feeling...

I believe that you are kind and incredible and creative in more ways than you know. My wish is that you discover, every day, in some way, just how wonderfully excellent you truly are.

Kindly & Creatively,

Here's to your excellence...

What's In Each Journal Entry

Each journal entry has four parts to it:

1. A thought for the day — things like words of advice and helpful reminders.

2. Qualities, traits and talents — where you and your buddies write down things that you like about each other (there are instructions and an example on the following pages).

3. A focus word for the day — an idea to explore or simply a word to think about. You can talk about it, write about it, draw a picture about it... or you can choose to do nothing about it. It's up to you!

4. Blank pages — some are lined and some are not. These pages are for your thoughts and feelings, or your drawings, art, poetry or any other creative journaling ideas that you might want to try. **What you think** and **how you feel** is important. And how you **choose to express** your thoughts and feelings is totally up to you! Remember, there are tons of creative journaling ideas on pages 24 - 31 to experiment with. You can journal about the thought for the day, the focus word, what's happening in your life, or anything else that you want to investigate or remember. You can even have your buddy write or draw in your journal if you like.

Looking for the Good Stuff

This is the part of the book where you will need the help of a journal buddy. There are four simple steps:

1. Choose your buddy.

2. Ask your buddy to pick three qualities, traits or talents that he admires about you and record them in your journal.

3. Next, it's your turn to pick three qualities, traits or talents that you admire about your buddy and record them in your journal.

4. Try to pick new qualities, traits and talents each time, and try not to repeat any choices that have already been used. Ask someone for help if you need new ideas, or look in a thesaurus! You can also look at the list on page 22.

And just so you know... this journal will be just a little glimpse of all your incredible qualities, traits and talents that go on and on forever!

Example of a Journal Entry

Journal Entry  17

Today's buddy is: *Jerry*

Today's date is: *September 23*

> *Focusing on your positive qualities, traits and talents takes a lot of courage.*

List three qualities, traits or talents that your buddy loves, likes or enjoys about you!

1. *He's smart.*
2. *kind*
3. *really funny*

List three qualities, traits or talents that you love, like or enjoy about your buddy!

1. *He's good at sports.*
2. *outgoing*
3. *tells great jokes*

> *And, courage is what makes a lion's roar a ROAR!*

 99

Qualities, Traits and Talents

Here are a few ideas of some qualities, traits and talents that you might want to use. If you don't know what a word means, look it up in the dictionary or ask someone to explain it to you. Remember to ASK FOR HELP if you need more ideas.

Qualities and Traits

funny	patient	creative	strong
smart	happy	confident	witty
gentle	lovable	wonderful	spontaneous
playful	imaginative	cheerful	determined
outgoing	curious	truthful	brave
courageous	independent	caring	fair
friendly	sweet	helpful	inspiring
nice	loyal	kind	intuitive
inventive	energetic	flexible	positive
sensitive	dependable	clever	understanding

Talents

singing	acting	writing	talking
drawing	academics	leading	storytelling
swimming	poetry	telling jokes	being silly
sports	giggling	inventing	building
planting	organizing	listening	playing
rhyming	cooking	dancing	piano
hanging out	making friends	making up games	cheering me up

RULES!

There are three rules that you must follow.

Rule One:

Criticism and put-downs are not allowed!

Rule Two:

Do your best to complete the journal. Complete an entry every day,
or skip a day, or do TWO journal entries in ONE day.
However you do it, just finish the journal.

Rule Three:

Have fun, have fun, have fun (and then have even MORE fun)
discovering and sharing your excellence!!!!!!!!!!!!!!

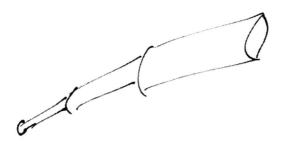

89 Creative Journaling Ideas

Below is a list of creative ways to make your journal keeping more enjoyable, personal, creative & fun. Some of the ideas require a computer and a printer. But if you can't print things at home, that's okay! Lots of kids don't have computers and printers at home. You could use a computer or printer at school, at the library, community center or ask a friend or relative for help. Besides, there are a gazillion other ways to be creative without computers... Dive in!

11. Summarize your day in 20 words or less.

2. Write one word across the journal page that best describes your day.

3. Write out the lyrics to your favorite song or print them out and paste them into your journal.

4. Draw a picture.

5. Write a poem.

6. Break all those writing and grammar rules and journal in your own unique style.

7. Print out a copy of an Instant Message chat that you had with your friend or your parent, and paste it into your journal.

8. Compose a song.

9. Write in your journal with markers, colored pencils or even crayons.

10. Cut and paste your favorite pictures from magazines into your journal.

11. Paste craft items into your journal (check with your Mom, aunts, or teachers for things you can use).

12. Brighten your journal with paint.

13. Paste stickers in your journal.

14. Include quotations by your favorite famous person, or someone you admire. You can find quotes online or in books from the library.

15. Record important events in history.

16. Draw a cartoon.

17. Record important news from the day.

18. Figure out how many days are left until your 13th birthday or your 16th birthday or your 18th, 21st, 33rd, 47th, 53rd or 111th birthday!

19. Interview a family member and record the interview in your journal.

20. Interview a friend and record the interview in your journal.

21. Write down 3 things that you're thankful for.

22. Write down 3 things that really bug you.

23. Invent a cool, new saying and record in your journal how and when you used it.

24. Invent an animal that no one except you has ever thought of before.

25. Draw a picture of an animal that no one except you has ever seen.

26. Go on a scavenger hunt and collect treasures from junk drawers, toy chests or other places and paste them into your journal.

27. Write a scavenger list of items you want to find that day, the next day, or that week, and record the results in your journal of when and how you found them.

28. Research your hero (historical, musical, sports...) and find similarities between your hero and you.

29. Imagine a wacky, weird or silly news headline about your day.

30. Write a news story about your day and use your imagination to add outrageous details.

31. Imagine the world you wish you could live in right now, then write about it or draw a picture of it.

32. Imagine you're a superhero and you had to save the world today. Write the story of how it happened or draw a picture of your superhero costume.

33. Look for cloud shapes online (or in the sky!) and describe or draw what you see in that cloud shape.

34. Create a flag design just for you.

35. Create a flag design for your family, friends, school or community.

36. Print out a map of a place that you want to visit someday and write about why you want to go there.

37. Make up an invention of your own and draw it or write about it. Use your imagination and give yourself permission to create something wild and crazy!

38. Make a paper snowflake and paste it into your journal.

39. Make a paper airplane and paste it into your journal.

40. Write out 10 predictions about your life in 3 months or 6 months, a year, or even 5, 10, 25 or 50 years...

41. Find a special recipe and prepare it for someone and write about the experience. Write the recipe in your journal.

42. Write an ad about yourself that explains why you're a great kid, son, friend, or student.

43. Look up the definition of a word that you don't know and write a story, song or poem about the word.

44. Look up the definition of a word that you don't know and draw a picture about it.

45. Make a list of your best life memories.

46. Compile a menu of your dream dinner.

47. List your favorite foods.

48. Write a letter to your grandparents or someone else who means a lot to you, and then paste a copy into your journal (don't forget to mail the letter if you want!).

49. Cut and paste articles from your local newspaper (or from news sites online) and explain why they're important to you.

50. Print out a special email from a parent, friend or grandparent and paste it into your journal.

51. Find information online about your favorite anything (book, sports figure, hero...) and print out the information or a picture of it, and paste it into your journal.

52. Take scraps of construction paper and paste them into your journal to create your own unique design.

53. Paint with watercolors in your journal, and don't worry if the pages get wavy from the water!

54. Cut out a page from a coloring book or print out a coloring page of something that you love from the internet. Color it and paste it into your journal.

55. Make a collage of your favorite photos of you, your family or your friends.

56. Look back at your journal entries, find your favorite one, and write about why it's your favorite entry. You might even try to create a second version of the entry, but with a new topic.

57. Ask your art teacher for scraps of paper or other "junk" he was planning to throw away. Find creative ways to paste this "junk" into your journal.

58. Go on a nature walk and search for weird things you wouldn't usually notice and record them in your journal.

59. Go on a treasure hunt outside, look for any little treasures — a leaf, small stone, or just a small scrap of something that is a cool color — and paste them into your journal. Try making up a story about your treasures!

60. Find something in your house or at school that would usually go in the trash — make sure it's clean and safe — and think of a creative way to use it in your journal.

61. Look up a creative writing prompt and use it to create a journal entry, or make up your own writing prompt. Two examples of creative writing prompts are "What would you do with 3 wishes?" or "If I were a _____ I would...."

62. Write a story or draw a picture from the point of view of a mouse going down a hole, or of a flower with a bee on it.

63. Make up your own secret language and write a journal entry about it.

64. What is your wildest dream? Write about it, draw a picture about it, or make up a poem or a song about it.

65. Find a spot to sit, look around and pick 5 things you can see and write about them or draw them in your journal.

66. Imagine that you're holding a magic pen in your hand right now. What can it do for you?

67. Ask at least five people you know to write one sentence about a topic of your choice (dogs, sports, games, pink elephants). Compile the sentences into a silly story.

68. Complete a journal entry using only pictures that you cut out of magazines, the newspaper or printed from the internet.

69. Do a word-play by writing out a single word, like "writing" and find as many words within that word as you can. In the word "writing" I can find: twin, grit, win, grin, wig, and tin — just to name a few!

70. Take a word and create another word or sentence for each letter of that word. So for the word "Kiss", you could write Keep It Simple Silly.

71. Record your favorite jokes in your journal or make up your own.

72. Find a special symbol or make one up and write or draw about it in your journal.

73. Write your goals for the day, week, and year, or even some for when you grow up.

74. Write things to do and special things that you want to remember from that day, week or year.

75. Have countdowns in your journal to birthdays, special trips or events.

76. Find a great poem and copy it into your journal.

77. Record everything you ate that day.

78. Spray perfume, cologne or some other scent on the pages and then write about what is special about this scent and why.

79. Record how much money you have, how much money you want, or how much money you dream about having when you grow up.

80. Tape money into your journal and do not spend it until a set date, or keep it as a reward for when you complete the journal.

81. Make a list of the things that you want to be, do or have that week.

82. Make a list of the things that you want to be, do or have when you grow up.

83. Make a list of things that you want to do with your family or your friends sometime this year.

84. Paste special letters or cards that you receive (birthday or holiday cards) into your journal.

85. Write a list of your favorite things.

86. Invent at least 10 new ways to sign your name, then choose your favorite new signature and use it for the next week.

87. Create a family chart and go back at least 3 generations, if not more. Ask your mom, dad or grandparent for help.

88. Make up your own word, give it a definition, and use it in a conversation.

and, finally... my favorite Creative Journaling idea!!!!!!!

89. Freely share your journal with others and ask them to write or draw in it.

There is simply no such thing as right or wrong when it comes to creative journaling. You can draw pictures, maps or secret symbols about your day. Write a song or a story about traveling in space! On one day, just write or just draw. Or on another day, do both! Remember, it's your journal and your choice. Come back to this list any time and try one of the ideas! And by the way, you can also find creative ways to journal about things that make you sad, things that upset you and things that are difficult to deal with. It doesn't have to always be happy. In fact, sometimes using creativity to express difficult emotions is easier to do than just plain old writing or talking about it. Sometimes, it can even help you feel better.

If you think of more ideas for creative journaling, make a list right here:

1.
2.
3.
4.
5.
6.
7.
8.
9.
10.
11.
12.
13.
14.
15.

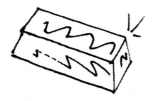

And now, you begin your journaling adventure...

Journal Entry

Today's buddy is:

Today's date is:

> *Every single person has a treasure chest filled with all sorts of qualities, traits and talents.*

List three qualities, traits or talents that your buddy loves, likes or enjoys about you!

1. ....

2. ....

3. ....

List three qualities, traits or talents that you love, like or enjoy about your buddy!

1. ....

2. ....

3. ....

> *Dig deeply to discover your treasures. Then dig even deeper to discover more!*

Today's focus word is: *Treasures*

Journal Entry

2

Today's buddy is:

Today's date is:

It's the positive stuff you like about YOURSELF that makes YOU feel proud.

List three qualities, traits or talents that your buddy loves, likes or enjoys about you!

1. ....

2. ....

3. ....

List three qualities, traits or talents that you love, like or enjoy about your buddy!

1. ....

2. ....

3. ....

What makes you feel proud about who you are?

Today's focus word is: Proud

Journal Entry

3

Today's buddy is:

Today's date is:

> Some people are shy, and others are bold. Some people are quiet, while others are loud. These differences are what make every single person sooooo special.

List three qualities, traits or talents that your buddy loves, likes or enjoys about you!

1.

2.

3.

List three qualities, traits or talents that you love, like or enjoy about your buddy!

1.

2.

3.

> Focusing on what makes you special will improve your confidence!

Today's focus word is: Confidence

Journal Entry

4

Today's buddy is:

Today's date is:

> *Anyone who says that it's not cool for boys to be nice and kind is very confused.*

List three qualities, traits or talents that your buddy loves, likes or enjoys about you!

1. ....

2. ....

3. ....

List three qualities, traits or talents that you love, like or enjoy about your buddy!

1. ....

2. ....

3. ....

> *After all, I happen to know — and I'm sure you do too — that there are tons of boys around who are nice and kind and cool.*

Today's focus word is: Kind

Journal Entry  5

Today's buddy is:

Today's date is:

> Words are powerful weapons that can build a person up or tear him down.

List three qualities, traits or talents that your buddy loves, likes or enjoys about you!

1.

2.

3.

List three qualities, traits or talents that you love, like or enjoy about your buddy!

1.

2.

3.

> And words, like weapons, must be used with great caution, skill and care. So do your best to speak, think and use positive words.

Today's focus word is: *Powerful*

Journal Entry

6

Today's buddy is:

Today's date is:

> *You act brave when you are kind toward others.*

List three qualities, traits or talents that your buddy loves, likes or enjoys about you!

1. ....

2. ....

3. ....

List three qualities, traits or talents that you love, like or enjoy about your buddy!

1. ....

2. ....

3. ....

> *psst... people who are mean to others are NOT brave. They're mean.*
>
> *psst... psst... are you brave enough to be kind to others?*

Today's focus word is: Brave

Journal Entry

7

Today's buddy is:

Today's date is:

> *Do you know that excellence on the inside shines through your eyes to the outside?*

List three qualities, traits or talents that your buddy loves, likes or enjoys about you!

1. ....
2. ....
3. ....

List three qualities, traits or talents that you love, like or enjoy about your buddy!

1. ....
2. ....
3. ....

> *By the way, sparkling, happy eyes are a great way to easily share your excellence with anyone and everyone!*

Today's focus word is: *Excellence*

Journal Entry

8

Today's buddy is:

Today's date is:

> With practice — just like with school, sports or video games — you'll feel more skilled at talking about the good stuff the more you do it.

List three qualities, traits or talents that your buddy loves, likes or enjoys about you!

1. ....

2. ....

3. ....

List three qualities, traits or talents that you love, like or enjoy about your buddy!

1. ....

2. ....

3. ....

> If you practice this a little bit everyday, you'll be skilled at looking for and finding (and talking about) the good stuff in no time.

Today's focus word is: PRACTICE

Journal Entry  9

Today's buddy is:

Today's date is:

> *Your imagination helps you to feel incredible, powerful and good.*

List three qualities, traits or talents that your buddy loves, likes or enjoys about you!

1. ....

2. ....

3. ....

List three qualities, traits or talents that you love, like or enjoy about your buddy!

1. ....

2. ....

3. ....

> *And by the way, it's also a great tool to help cheer yourself up if you're feeling sad or blue.*

Today's focus word is: Imagination

Journal Entry  10

Today's buddy is:

Today's date is:

> Self-esteem is how you feel about yourself and knowing that you are valuable in everyway.

List three qualities, traits or talents that your buddy loves, likes or enjoys about you!

1. ....

2. ....

3. ....

List three qualities, traits or talents that you love, like or enjoy about your buddy!

1. ....

2. ....

3. ....

> You can build and strengthen your self-esteem by focusing on the positives and feeling proud of your unique self.

Today's focus word is: Self-esteem

Journal Entry 11

Today's buddy is:

Today's date is:

> *Do your best to challenge yourself to find the good in others.*

List three qualities, traits or talents that your buddy loves, likes or enjoys about you!

1.

2.

3.

List three qualities, traits or talents that you love, like or enjoy about your buddy!

1.

2.

3.

> *Sometimes this can be difficult. But, keep looking and I promise you that you'll find at least one thing that you like about everyone.*

Today's focus word is: Challenge

Journal Entry

12

Today's buddy is:

Today's date is:

> *CELEBRATE the new discoveries that you uncover about yourself and others for a little while each and every day.*

List three qualities, traits or talents that your buddy loves, likes or enjoys about you!

1. _____

2. _____

3. _____

List three qualities, traits or talents that you love, like or enjoy about your buddy!

1. _____

2. _____

3. _____

> *Remember to share your discoveries with others!*

Today's focus word is: *Discoveries*

Journal Entry  13

Today's buddy is:

Today's date is:

> *You get to choose how you treat others and who to have as friends.*

List three qualities, traits or talents that your buddy loves, likes or enjoys about you!

1. _____

2. _____

3. _____

List three qualities, traits or talents that you love, like or enjoy about your buddy!

1. _____

2. _____

3. _____

> *So, act carefully and choose wisely.*

Today's focus word is: *Choose*

Journal Entry

14

Today's buddy is:

Today's date is:

> *If something doesn't work for you the first time you try it, simply try again and then again and then AGAIN until it works for you.*

List three qualities, traits or talents that your buddy loves, likes or enjoys about you!

1. ....

2. ....

3. ....

List three qualities, traits or talents that you love, like or enjoy about your buddy!

1. ....

2. ....

3. ....

> *That's called determination!*

Today's focus word is: DETERMINATION

Journal Entry

15

Today's buddy is:

Today's date is:

> If someone is being mean to you or if you're being bullied, it's okay to reach out to others and ask for help.

List three qualities, traits or talents that your buddy loves, likes or enjoys about you!

1. _____

2. _____

3. _____

List three qualities, traits or talents that you love, like or enjoy about your buddy!

1. _____

2. _____

3. _____

> You can reach out to a friend, parent, grandparent, teacher, neighbor or to any grown-up you trust.

Today's focus word is: Help

Journal Entry

16

Today's buddy is:

Today's date is:

> What you think about yourself is important.
> I mean it... what YOU think about YOURSELF
> is the most important thing in the whole wide world!

List three qualities, traits or talents that your buddy loves, likes or enjoys about you!

1. ....
2. ....
3. ....

List three qualities, traits or talents that you love, like or enjoy about your buddy!

1. ....
2. ....
3. ....

> So try and think more about the stuff that makes you
> so wonderfully excellent.

Today's focus word is: Important

Journal Entry

17

Today's buddy is:

Today's date is:

> Focusing on your positive qualities, traits and talents takes a lot of courage.

List three qualities, traits or talents that your buddy loves, likes or enjoys about you!

1.

2.

3.

List three qualities, traits or talents that you love, like or enjoy about your buddy!

1.

2.

3.

> And, courage is what makes a lion's roar a ROAR!

Today's focus word is: Courage

Journal Entry  18

Today's buddy is:

Today's date is:

Try to unlock all of your talents, especially those you've kept hidden away or maybe didn't even know about before.

List three qualities, traits or talents that your buddy loves, likes or enjoys about you!

1.

2.

3.

List three qualities, traits or talents that you love, like or enjoy about your buddy!

1.

2.

3.

psst... sometimes it's your hidden talents that are the most valuable and enjoyable of all. How can you unlock yours?

Today's focus word is: Valuable

Journal Entry

Today's buddy is:

Today's date is:

> *It's amazingly and outrageously fun to hold your head high and speak about the positives.*

List three qualities, traits or talents that your buddy loves, likes or enjoys about you!

1. _____
2. _____
3. _____

List three qualities, traits or talents that you love, like or enjoy about your buddy!

1. _____
2. _____
3. _____

> *It's also a great way to show respect to yourself and others!*

Today's focus word is: Respect

Journal Entry  20

Today's buddy is:

Today's date is:

> *It takes a warrior's spirit to focus on the stuff you like about yourself and others.*

List three qualities, traits or talents that your buddy loves, likes or enjoys about you!

1. ....

2. ....

3. ....

List three qualities, traits or talents that you love, like or enjoy about your buddy!

1. ....

2. ....

3. ....

> *A true warrior knows he should always do the right thing, not just what other people want him to do.*

Today's focus word is: WARRIOR

Journal Entry

21

Today's buddy is:

Today's date is:

Praise yourself in some way, everyday.

List three qualities, traits or talents that your buddy loves, likes or enjoys about you!

1. ....
2. ....
3. ....

List three qualities, traits or talents that you love, like or enjoy about your buddy!

1. ....
2. ....
3. ....

Then find a way to praise your buddies everyday too!

Today's focus word is: Praise

Journal Entry

22

Today's buddy is:

Today's date is:

> Looking for the positive and focusing on what you like about yourself and others will make you smile and laugh more.

List three qualities, traits or talents that your buddy loves, likes or enjoys about you!

1. ....
2. ....
3. ....

List three qualities, traits or talents that you love, like or enjoy about your buddy!

1. ....
2. ....
3. ....

> And that feels awesome. Why don't you try it right now?

Today's focus word is: Smile

Journal Entry

Today's buddy is:

Today's date is:

> You can be a baseball player, a carpenter, a teacher, a doctor, the President, or anything you dream of.

List three qualities, traits or talents that your buddy loves, likes or enjoys about you!

1. ....

2. ....

3. ....

List three qualities, traits or talents that you love, like or enjoy about your buddy!

1. ....

2. ....

3. ....

> What's your dream?

Today's focus word is: Dream

Journal Entry

24

Today's buddy is:

Today's date is:

If you ever feel lonely, remember your journal buddies.

List three qualities, traits or talents that your buddy loves, likes or enjoys about you!

1. ....

2. ....

3. ....

List three qualities, traits or talents that you love, like or enjoy about your buddy!

1. ....

2. ....

3. ....

Then, remember how much they love and admire you.

Today's focus word is: Admire

Journal Entry

25

Today's buddy is:

Today's date is:

> *Practice looking into a mirror and saying out loud the things you like about yourself.*

List three qualities, traits or talents that your buddy loves, likes or enjoys about you!

1. ....

2. ....

3. ....

List three qualities, traits or talents that you love, like or enjoy about your buddy!

1. ....

2. ....

3. ....

> *Then try it again with a smile and some laughter (or a chuckle)!*

Today's focus word is: Laughter

Journal Entry

26

Today's buddy is:

Today's date is:

> Sometimes other people's mean words or mean actions hook onto us and grab our attention, even though we don't want them to.

List three qualities, traits or talents that your buddy loves, likes or enjoys about you!

1. ....

2. ....

3. ....

List three qualities, traits or talents that you love, like or enjoy about your buddy!

1. ....

2. ....

3. ....

> If this happens to you, just try to remember that you CAN and WILL find a way to free yourself from their hook.

Today's focus word is: Free

Journal Entry

27

Today's buddy is:

Today's date is:

> *Everyone makes mistakes or fails sometimes.*

List three qualities, traits or talents that your buddy loves, likes or enjoys about you!

1. ....

2. ....

3. ....

List three qualities, traits or talents that you love, like or enjoy about your buddy!

1. ....

2. ....

3. ....

> *That's how we learn and grow!*

Today's focus word is: GROW

Journal Entry  28

Today's buddy is:

Today's date is:

> *Celebrate your good stuff.*
> *Then celebrate your buddies' good stuff.*

List three qualities, traits or talents that your buddy loves, likes or enjoys about you!

1. ....

2. ....

3. ....

List three qualities, traits or talents that you love, like or enjoy about your buddy!

1. ....

2. ....

3. ....

> *Then celebrate even more good stuff about yourself, your*
> *friend, your parent, your pet... anyone you can think of!*

Today's focus word is: Celebrate

Journal Entry  29

Today's buddy is:

Today's date is:

> *It takes great strength just to be YOU.*

List three qualities, traits or talents that your buddy loves, likes or enjoys about you!

1. ....

2. ....

3. ....

List three qualities, traits or talents that you love, like or enjoy about your buddy!

1. ....

2. ....

3. ....

> *And the more you discover and know about YOURSELF, the more strength you'll have!*

Today's focus word is: STRENGTH

Journal Entry  30

Today's buddy is:

Today's date is:

> *Being comfortable expressing and sharing your excellent self is a precious gift that you can give to yourself.*

List three qualities, traits or talents that your buddy loves, likes or enjoys about you!

1.

2.

3.

List three qualities, traits or talents that you love, like or enjoy about your buddy!

1.

2.

3.

> *This is a super-amazing gift to give to others, too!*

Today's focus word is: Gift

Wahooooooooooo!

Congratulations - you're done with the journal entries!

Up next, the section for reflection.

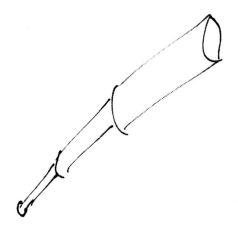

Section for Reflection

Before you're completely done with this journal, there are a few more super fun and really valuable activities for you to do. On the following pages, you will reflect on your journaling adventure and record some final thoughts about yourself, your buddies and your *Journal Buddies* experience.

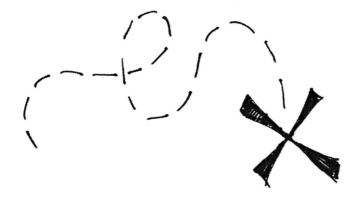

Your Favorite Qualities, Traits and Talents

Go back through your journal and look at the qualities, traits and talents that you wrote for each entry. What are your favorite 10 excellent characteristics that YOUR BUDDIES chose about YOU?

1. ....

2. ....

3. ....

4. ....

5. ....

6. ....

7. ....

8. ....

9. ....

10. ....

What are your favorite 10 excellent characteristics that YOU chose about YOUR BUDDIES?

1. ....

2. ....

3. ....

4. ....

5. ....

6. ....

7. ....

8. ....

9. ....

10. ....

Now choose the top THREE qualities, traits and talents that you like the MOST about you and about your buddies, and circle or put a star next to them or highlight them in whatever way you wish.

Your Favorite
Journal Entries

Now review all 30 journal entries and pick your favorite one. Write about why it's your favorite. Or instead, choose a whole bunch of favorite entries and write about why you like them! There could be all kinds of reasons why you really like a journal entry. Maybe you really love a picture that you drew, or something that your buddy said about you, or a poem that you wrote, or the thought for the day. Whatever it is, just have fun with it!

The Buddies I Admire Most and Why

List the buddy or buddies that you admire the most. Do you feel differently about your buddies now that you've completed this journal? Do you see them differently? Describe any differences and use lots of details to help you think about your experience.

What You've Learned About Yourself

What are some of the best things that you learned about yourself while completing this journal? Do you feel differently about yourself? Do you see yourself differently? Describe any differences, and again, use lots of details to help you think about your experience.

Bravo!
Way to go!
Well done!
You did it!

One Final Thought

You can discover and share excellence anywhere you find it. Whatever you love, like or enjoy about your buddies, yourself, or anyone or anything... you can talk about it, write about it, or draw a picture about it. You can make up a dance, a play, a song, or a poem about it. You can notice it quietly and feel it in your bones. You can laugh about it, smile about it, or even yell out loud about it. The possibilities are endless!

I hope you enjoyed your journaling adventure and I want to congratulate you on a job well done! Most of all, I hope you keep this journal in a safe place where you can pick it up — again and again — and remind yourself of how amazing, incredible, creative, kind, special, magical and unique you truly are.

Again, here's to your excellence...

About the Author

Jill Schoenberg was born and raised in St. Cloud, Minnesota. She received a Bachelor of Science degree in Youth Studies and Sociology from the University of Minnesota. She is passionate about creating tools for kids to help them develop their self-esteem, and she loves creative journaling! Her professional experience includes more than seven years of working directly with young people — helping them to understand and strengthen their self-esteem, creative talents and life-skills.

Jill is an avid reader and journal writer. She loves horses, writing, nature walks, motorcycles, running and meditation, along with her wonderful and supportive family and friends. Oh, and she loves her cat, too! One of her favorite pastimes is savoring a breath-taking sunset and relishing the many joys of a painted sky. She currently lives next to a sparkling lake in north-central Minnesota.